HOW TO BE THE MASTER OF THE UNIVERSE

MIKE NACH

Copyright © 2014 Mike Nach
All rights reserved.
ISBN-13:978-1502721907
ISBN-10: 1502721902

THE TABLE OF CONTENTS

DISCLAIMER 1
INTRODUCTION 3
PART I 9
OUR HOLOGRAPHIC UNIVERSE 11
POWERS OF ENLIGHTENMENT 13
HOW TO BE DETACHED 17
    1: MANIFESTATION 18
    2: GOALS 19
    3: LOST OPPORTUNITIES 19
    4: RELATIONSHIPS 20
    5: SEX 21

THE SELF OR BODY OF LIGHT 23
THE "SELFIE" EXPERIMENTS 25
    EXPERIMENT 1: THE HAPPINESS TEST 26
    EXPERIMENT 2: THE "BEFORE" AND "AFTER" PHOTOS TEST 28
    EXPERIMENT 3: THE BODY OF LIGHT EXERCISE 29
    EXPERIMENT 4: BEING YOUR REAL SELF 30
    EXPERIMENT 5: SILENCING THE MIND 31
    EXPERIMENT 6: MIND FEEDBACK 32
    EXPERIMENT 7: MIND CONTROL 33

TESTING THE POWERS OF THE SELF 35
    1: HOW TO MANIFEST PHYSICAL OBJECTS 36
    2: HOW TO ATTRACT YOUR SOUL MATE 38
    3: HOW TO HEAL YOURSELF 40
    4: HOW TO CHANGE YOUR PRESENT SITUATION 43
    5: HOW TO HANDLE PROBLEMATIC PEOPLE AT THE OFFICE 45
    6: HOW TO HANDLE VICIOUS PEOPLE 47
    7: HOW TO DEAL WITH THE FEAR OF DEATH 48

PART II 51
ASHTAVAKRA GITA 51
ASHTAVAKRA AND KING JANAKA 53

1: Instant Liberation 56
2: What's real? 57
3: The Power of True Knowledge 59
4: The Dissolution of Consciousness....................................60
5: The Limitless Ocean of the Self..62
6: Bondage and Freedom 63
7: Indifference...65
8: Dispassion...66
9: Pure and Radiant Self 67
10: Supreme Knowledge 68
11: Awakening!...69

THANK YOU! 73
MY BOOKS 74

DISCLAIMER

The author and publisher have used their best efforts in preparing this book. Every effort has been made to accurately represent the teachings / techniques mentioned in this book, and their potential. Your level of success in attaining the results claimed in this book depends on the correct usage of the teachings and techniques given and the time you devote to the techniques and ideas given.

Since these factors differ according to individuals, we cannot guarantee your success. Nor are we responsible for any of your actions. Consulting a competent professional is advisable.

The author and publisher shall in no event be held liable to any party for any direct, indirect, punitive, special, psychological, incidental or other consequential damages arising, directly or indirectly, from any use of this material, which is provided "as is", and without warranties.

If you wish to apply the ideas contained in this book, you're taking full responsibility for your action.

INTRODUCTION

A lot of water has flowed under the bridge since I published my Kindle ebook **"HOW TO GET ANYTHING YOU WANT? MAKE A MAGICK MIRROR!"** http://ASIN.cc/RahVJf It was a very satisfying experience. Numerous readers contacted me to tell me that my book helped them a lot. I am very pleased that my book was able to help them. It has changed my life in many wondrous ways, too!

Ever since childhood, I was fascinated by tales of genies and magick mirrors. I was very envious of Aladdin. This guy had a magick ring as well as a magick lamp. He had to rub the ring or the lamp and, "voila," out came a genie to grant his wishes.

I would close my eyes and dream-

"If I had either the magick ring or the lamp, how lucky would I be?"

"I would wish for a billion dollars, mansions, planes, yachts and other goodies."

"I would have beautiful girls by my side." And so on.

These daydreams were never ending. You know, what I mean?

I was aware that most fairy tales had a ring of truth about them. I decided to research the subject of magickal manifestation. After reading countless books and browsing the internet, I finally homed on to the magick mirror. Here was a powerful occult tool which would help manifest anything I wanted. It would be my magickal ring or lamp. I constructed the magick mirror and tried it. Believe it or not, it worked. I was able to manifest money and material possessions in the shortest possible time. I was excited. I was in possession of a very potent manifestation device. I wanted to spread the word. I wanted everybody to experience the power. So, I wrote the above book.

After a while, I started feeling restless. Hankering after money, material possessions or human relationships is not my primary goal in life. I wanted knowledge. I wanted to dive into the unknown and discover what's there. I prayed to the universe to help me out. It did! My gaze fell on a tiny book on my bookshelf. I pulled it out. The title of the book was unpronounceable- **ASHTAVAKRA GITA**. This book was an English translation, of an ancient Indian metaphysical manuscript, by an Indian author, *Radhakamal Mukerjee*. I was intrigued. When did I buy this book? I don't remember. There are many titles on my bookshelf and in my e reader which I have not read. I buy whichever title grabs my attention thinking I will read it afterwards, but I never do.

Maybe this book had the answers to my restless mind. I started reading it. At first, I was not able to figure out what the two protagonists, **Sage Ashtavakra** and **King Janaka**, were saying. I read it a couple of times before the teachings began to sink in. I was hooked. These guys were talking a lot of sense.

Questions like –

"Who are we?"

"What's our true purpose in life?"

"Who created this universe?"

"Who is God?"

"What is manifestation?"

"What's the magical key to manifestation and enlightenment?"

"How to be truly happy (enlightened)?"

are answered in a straight forward manner. No allegorical language. My mind was reeling! This book was awesome. Here was a new and simple way to get anything you want! No elaborate rituals, visualization or meditative practices were necessary for manifestation.

I followed their advice. It worked. I could manifest anything I wanted. I was also becoming very peaceful. My mind had become calm. I literally changed overnight. People noticed my changed appearance and inquired about it. I smiled. It was working. I wanted to share this knowledge with the world.

I bought other versions of the Ashtavakra Gita and read them like a man possessed. Each had its good points, but none of them would appeal to normal folks, like you and me. I decided to write an easily understandable version of this ancient treatise. I have written this book as I have understood it.

Follow the guidelines and your life will never be the same again. You will never again feel, "This world sucks." You will never be hurt by any bad incident in your life. You can have anything you want easily and miraculously. You will feel blissful. You will lead a very satisfied life. This is not a rehash of the Law of Attraction books floating around. Okay, okay, you check it out and tell me whether I am just babbling and trying to sell my book or there's something to it.

So, what's this Ashtavakra Gita about?

The Ashtavakra Gita is a conversation (in the form of verses) between Ashtavakra, a great self realized being, and King Janaka, known for his wisdom. Some historians have opined that it was written around 500-400 BCE while others feel that it came a good deal later- eight or the fourteenth century. Whatever! Let's not argue over it. It's pretty old, anyway.

The original treatise consists of 298 stanzas and each of these stanzas has sufficient information to transport a seeker instantaneously to the ultimate destination (from mental bondage to liberation) without much effort. You don't need to cultivate any particular qualities nor renounce your current lifestyle. There are neither suggestions for self improvement nor rules for social behavior. Ashtavakra stresses that you don't need a guru to understand the supreme truth. If you know the basic rules then you can DIY at home. This advice is a game changer!

However, the original text cannot be easily understood by those whose minds have been not been conditioned to understand metaphysical concepts. I have tried my best to make the original verses understandable and concise. This is a condensed version of the Ashtavakra Gita.

Many ancient teachings were couched in metaphorical language. You need to literally read between the lines to understand what the author wants to convey. Not so, with Ashtavakra. He is a man in a hurry. He has no time for poetry or window dressing. He wants to dish it out straight.

He advises us to recognize our true identity as the Self, or pure awareness. We are immortal souls or the Self. We are God. We are all equal. This universe is an illusion. Our minds have created it and given it a separate identity. This universe and everything in it is illusory and has arisen from the minds of the collective souls present in all beings (infinite consciousness). The thought "I" has created this duality and we, in our ignorance, think of this material world as real and try to sustain it. This book will not only teach you how to live with this illusion but it will literally change your life around. You will never be the same individual again.

We are prisoners of our creation! We need to be desireless. This secret will give us an edge. We have the power to create anything with our minds and also renounce it if we so desire.

The key ideas of the Ashtavakra Gita have been repeated many, many times in this book. I have not done it to fill the pages. They are affirmations which you (Self) and the mind need to accept and act accordingly. Reading a particular topic, a few times, allows the mind to soak the information in and retain it.

This book is divided into two parts-

Part I deals with concepts given in the Ashtavakra Gita and how you can use this knowledge to have anything you want and also become very peaceful.

Part II has the story of how the Sage Ashtavakra and King Janaka became friends, followed by their spiritual discourse, the Ashtavakra Gita.

PART I

Can you see the faint image of the Body of Light?

3-D Universe painted on a 2-D cosmological surface (horizon)

HOLOGRAPHIC UNIVERSE

OUR HOLOGRAPHIC UNIVERSE

If you ask a person on the street, "What's this universe made of?"

You will most probably be told, "Matter and energy."

A quantum physicist would answer, "Everything in this universe is pure energy vibrating at different rates." Some theoretical scientists would counter, "This physical universe is made of information."

There's also a theory called **"the holographic principle."** According to this principle- the universe, which we consider to be three-dimensional, could be "painted" on a two-dimensional cosmological surface (horizon), like a **hologram**. It's similar to recordings of three dimensional images on a two-dimensional flat surface like paper, film, TV, movie, computer screens etc. Take our earth for example. It's a gigantic ovoid shaped three-dimensional planet. However, the land on which we are standing appears flat or two-dimensional. Didn't our ancestors feel that the earth was flat and we could fall off the edge if we ventured there?

Some physicists are even saying that the so called **"Dark Energy,"** an unknown force which is accelerating the expansion of this universe, could also be an illusion.

All these scientific conjectures are changing our perceptions about our universe.

Our universe is a profound illusion! Intriguing!

Is this not what ancient Indian sages, like Ashtavakra and King Janaka, had been shouting from the roof tops?

Everything's a grand illusion created by our minds!

We are living in the matrix- a world created by our minds. It's generated by the collective minds of all beings in the infinite consciousness. It's safe to conclude that time and space never really exists, nor existed. All of it is our creation! We are God!

We are experiencing a gigantic reality show of universal proportions. We are the producers, directors, actors, technicians and spectators of this spectacular show. Some of us are playing spectacular roles in this illusory show. Some have taken "loser" roles. There's no authority to tell us what roles are suitable for us. Then, why have many of us chosen unsatisfactory roles? Why play a particular role if you do not like it? What's stopping you? Talk to your mind and demand a better role. You deserve it for playing along with your mind.

You have three choices to do anything you want.

1: Be a bystander- Ashtavakra recommends that you don't take an active part in this cosmic soap opera. Be a bystander. He exhorts you to remember your true Self and not be a prisoner of your creation. He wants you to be free from the problems you will be facing while playing your role. This should ideally be everyone's true goal in life. Why take part in roles which imprisons you and makes you feel lousy at some time or the other? It's your take!

2: Role playing with detachment- You can be a winner in this cosmic show if you are totally detached. Play your role with detachedness. If you are desireless, you will attain all your desires. You will be unaffected by the ups and downs of this illusory world. How? I will be discussing this ahead.

3: Role playing with total involvement- Okay, if you want to take an active part in this illusory show, then why the heck don't you change your script? Refuse loser roles. Tell your mind to shut up. Erase the role you don't want. Plan a better script for yourself. You can have anything you want! You can be a superhero!

The choice is yours. Choose wisely.

POWERS OF ENLIGHTENMENT

Enlightenment is about understanding the illusory nature of the material world and knowing what reality really is. If you grasp the truth about what everything is, and what it really means to have something, then you can have anything you want. That's enlightenment. It's a pity that most people don't realize that you need to be enlightened before you are able to successfully manifest material things in your life.

It's true. Ashtavakra and King Janaka said it thousands of years ago.

The desireless attain all their desires.

What does it mean to be desireless? Does it mean that you should have no desires?

No! It means that you should have no attachment to desire. Attachment is the cause of all suffering. If you want to end your suffering then you need to let go of all attachments. When you are attached, you will always lack or want something. If you are not attached to anything, you are in a state of being desireless. It is this detached state which gets you what you desire.

Let me explain.

According to Ashtavakra, this universe and everything present in it is illusory and created by our collective minds in the infinite consciousness. If the universe is our creation, it means everything in it already belongs to us. Our minds, due to preconditioning, have created this illusion of lack but in reality, the thing we desire is always with us. You have the power to manifest anything which is present in this illusory universe. If you remember this truth, you will become detached, because you know that you already have what you want. On the other hand, if you are obsessed and keep on thinking that you don't have a particular object of your desire, then it's disbelieving the universal truth. It will not manifest in your life.

Ashtavakra has emphasized that if you want to be truly free then you need to be detached and understand your true Self. Most people don't get what they want because they haven't freed themselves to possess it. They feel that they should get a particular thing in the manner they want, and no other way. Don't be choosy. Be detached. Allow your mind to find a way to grant your wish. **Detachment from choice is the secret of success.**

Enlightened manifestation of your desires will help you enjoy anything you like in life, and also be satisfied. You will be more successful in every field of life than others who do not follow this principle.

If you are detached, you will automatically become successful and happier than those who are mired in desires and wants. When you are being detached, you are resonating with having. When you are being attached, you are resonating with lack. There's an old saying ***"You will be able to get whatever you want only after you no longer need it."*** This doesn't mean you don't want it, but you are nonplussed about wanting it.

Most of us feel that we will be truly happy if we become rich, successful and get everything we desire. That's not true. We have not understood what true happiness is about.

According to Ashtavakra, if we realize this material world is illusory and a creation of our collective minds in the infinite consciousness, then we become truly peaceful. It's a state where we can manifest anything we want. When we have no attachments, our happiness is permanent.

Detachment is the magical key to manifestation and enlightenment.

An unenlightened person may ask what enlightenment has got to becoming rich or getting the love interest of your dreams. The answer is everything. When you are enlightened, you realize that it's not about manifesting your desires, but it's all about knowing what reality is (illusory creation), and who you really are (Self). If you grasp this knowledge then you are free to create whatever you wish. You will be happy, confident, free, peaceful and empowered.

You can amuse yourself by treating this illusory world as a game and play with illusions (manifest anything you want) without being ensnared by it.

You will be the true creator of the universe!

HOW TO BE DETACHED

In the previous chapter we discussed a bit about detachment. Let's delve further.

Sage Ashtavakra has repeatedly reminded us that this universe and everything in it is illusory and a creation of our mind. There's only one truth-the Self. If you realize this, it will be easy for you to detach ourselves from the ups and downs of this world and be truly peaceful. This is okay if you do not wish to take part in the cosmic game. But, what if you wish to take part in this game, then how do you remain detached?

Let's suppose you (Self) want to manifest something in your life. **Be detached to the outcome.** Realize that your mind has the power to create anything for you. Being attached to the outcome means that you have no trust in your mind's abilities of creation; you have doubts, fear or desires which produce the opposite effect. If you become attached, it means you are looking to other sources than your mind to fulfill your desires. These negative emotions prevent you to create the things you want. **Attachment will always create a feeling of want no matter how much of it you already have.** You will feel insecure and always have thoughts of not getting or losing the thing you desire. This attitude causes much unhappiness.

Learn to trust your mind. It knows how to manifest anything you want. You don't need to know the how's, why's and when you will receive the object of your desire. **Just state your intentions and desires and remain detached from the how and when they manifest. You will receive it!**

Have you ever noticed this- How many times have you got something you want when you were in an "I don't care" mood? Surprised at the answer? It's true!

You are able to manifest when you really don't seem to want it.

So, be detached.

Always remember you are playing a game. This game has been created by your mind and is not real. Don't be too attached with objects in this illusory game. Ask your mind to create it for you and expect it to happen. Suppose, it doesn't happen, then don't bother. Be detached. Maybe, the mind felt that your desire was not right. Or, it will give you something else which, in retrospect, was the right choice for you. Detachment doesn't mean you are indifferent nor have no feeling. It's a feeling of self realization that you have power over the thing you want and thus you need not be too attached to it.

When you are successfully detached from the outcome you realize you are able to create anything you want and are absolutely certain that all that you desire is already yours. If you, however, elect to remain attached then you will continue to focus on the negative aspects of what you don't want and have fears and doubts over your ability to manifest.

Always give your mind a choice about the thing you desire. Don't try to force your intention that you would want it in a certain way and no other way. You will create a roadblock. You are being attached. If you create several other options then you will definitely get what is right for you.

Let's figure out how to be detached in some daily life scenarios:

1: Manifestation- You (Self) must always remember that this is an illusory world and you are playing a role because of your mind. This universe and everything in it has been created by the collective minds of all beings. Since you have realized that you have the power to create anything you want, be detached to the outcome. You should lead your mind and not the other way around. If you need something, simply ask your mind to create it for you. Don't ponder about the how's, why's and the when's. **Give your mind the freedom of choice.** Don't force your mind by telling it that you want your desired object in a certain way and at a certain time.

You will surely receive what you have asked, in the perfect time and the perfect way.

2: Goals- Most LOA and self help books stress upon the important role of having goals in your life. What does "having goals" mean? It means that you have attached yourself to achieving a certain objective at a certain time. You have now become obsessed with results as a result of which you suffer anxiety and frustration. You will either worry a lot or tend to find quick-fix solutions if you are led astray from your intended goal.

Does this mean that you should set no goals?

No! Have goals. Try to achieve them. But, don't be attached to the outcome. Tell your mind about your goal and ask it to help you. Be assured you will achieve it in the right possible way.

You will surely achieve what you have set, in the perfect time and the perfect way.

3: Lost opportunities- Suppose you had gone for a job interview. It's a cinch. You feel you have created a favorable impression with your interviewers. It looks like you will get the job. What if there's a distance between the cup and the lip? Your dream job has landed on someone else's lap. What's your reaction? Rant? Are you going to feel the world has collapsed because you didn't get the job? Was this the last great job in this illusory world?

Be calm. Be detached. Tell yourself that another great opportunity is on its way. Ask your mind to direct this opportunity your way. After that, just switch off. No more questions or doubts on this topic.

You will surely receive what you have asked, in the perfect time and the perfect way.

You can try out this method for any other opportunities which you thought were coming your way, but didn't.

4: Relationships- Detachment is one of the ways of having a fulfilling relationship. Huh? Aren't relationships built on the "give and take", attachments and emotional platforms? Yes! At the same time, practicing detachment, while in a relationship, will benefit you greatly.

How do we go about it?

Well! Stop worrying! We tend to worry about our past and present relationships and about the future of our current relationship? Why connect the past to the present and future? Detach yourself from any fear or worry and be thankful for the present. This should melt your worries to a certain degree.

Don't think of the possible outcome of your current relationship. Remind yourself that you and your partner are playing the roles of lovers in this illusory cosmic opera. It's not real. Your true Self does not require outside relationships to make you happy. You don't need anybody to complete you. You are the Self who is perfect and complete in all ways. You are independent. If you realize this, you will feel empowered, enlightened, and grateful. This doesn't mean that you should stop being affectionate, loving or caring. It means you shouldn't feel powerless or think that you cannot live without your partner. That's attachment. Don't waste your time trying to look good, **feel good and be good** to attract a person. The other person will automatically sense that you are acting desperate and will wonder whether this person has no choices.

You also increase your chances with anyone if you show you are not attached to a response from him / her. Behave as if you don't need them. You will become more desirable because the other person has no way of figuring out the intensity of your affection.

Start loving your true inner Self. Since "like attracts like" You will attract a person who has also realized the Self. That will be the most fulfilling and the happiest relationship you will ever have.

5: Sex- Sex was created as a means of creating new physical bodies. This original purpose got lost on the way. Sex has now become a means of recreation.

Sex is one of the most powerful emotions which can make a person powerless. It's also the reason why the mind desires to play roles in this illusory world.

According to scientists, enjoyment of sex is not between the legs but between the ears.

The brain! I will substitute mind for the brain. It's the mind which has got used to sensual pleasures and this addiction can cause a lot of unhappiness and frustration.

The mind has equated sex with happiness and power. This illusion is the primary cause of unhappiness in the material world.

I am not against sex. It's very enjoyable! Hmm! Don't be concerned with the outcome. Don't worry about your organ size. Don't hanker after orgasms. Don't try to be a stud. All these feelings limit your true enjoyment. Use this opportunity to get to know the other Self who has participated with you in this union. Be detached. Don't dream about the pleasures which you may have experienced during the act. This will make you want to have sex all over again. You will never be free. Your mind will not be able to think clearly about other issues.

Sex is not just union of two bodies but also a union of two minds who have come together. Remember this; you (Self) are beyond sex and other illusory pleasures. The happiness which comes after you realize your true Self is immeasurable.

I have a **gross advice for sex addicts**. Guys, if you wish to cure your sex addiction then all you need to do is activate your X-ray vision. What's that? If you have been captivated by a certain individual and feel the strong desire to have sex with him/ her, then look at them with your X-ray eyes. See their skeletons. Now, do you still feel like having sex with the skeleton? Do this exercise whenever you feel the need to control your desires.

If you are interested in knowing more about desirelessness, happiness and the Game of Life, check out my book "Game of Life." You will be enlightened!

http://ASIN.cc/1Q7_D9W

https://www.createspace.com/5344252

THE SELF OR BODY OF LIGHT

Ashtavakra exhorts you to recognize your true identity. You are not this physical body. It's an illusion just like everything else. You are an immortal, unborn, timeless, luminous soul or the Self which is playing a role in this illusory world. **You are a part of the infinite consciousness.**

Eastern mystics say that the Self is subtler than space. It cannot be seen by your normal sight. It has no name and cannot be described. Neither the mind nor the senses can comprehend it. It's pure consciousness. The entire universe exists in the consciousness just like the blueprints of a plant exist in the seed. The Self is empty like space but it is not nothingness because it is consciousness. Its existence can be indirectly experienced just like the flower can be experienced by its fragrance.

Western occultists have called the Self the **"Body of Light (BoL)."** The BoL cannot be seen by the physical eyes but it can be seen by the psychic vision. Since the BoL is infinite intelligence it has a mind or thinking process. This mind present in every Self has enacted this cosmic soap opera and made the Self a prisoner. Since the mind and the Self cannot be separated, the Self is forced to play a role in this illusory world. Thus every "living" being has a Self and mind within it. This Self or BoL becomes egg shaped and permeates our body, protruding from it in all directions. This BoL is elastic and can take any shape as per the dictates of the mind.

Let's believe! This information is going to help us a lot.

THE "SELFIE" EXPERIMENTS

In the previous chapter, you learned a bit about yourself. You're not a physical body made of flesh and bones but a body of light (BoL) or the Self. This ignorance has caused you dearly. It's time to change your miserable condition and become what you truly are.

Immortal, powerful, detached and happy.

So, let's carry out a few experiments to get acquainted with your Self.

Experiment 1: The happiness test

If you recognize your true Self then you instinctively feel happy. This experiment will help you find out.

1: Take a diary and pencil. Write the date when you will begin this exercise. The title on top of the page will be- **THE HAPPINESS QUOTIENT**

2: Draw a line and divide it into seven equal parts.

1----------2----------3-----------4----------5----------6------------7

The happiness scale:

1= extremely unhappy

2= moderately unhappy

3= slightly unhappy

4= vacillates from unhappy to happy

5= slightly happy

6 = moderately happy

7 = very happy

How would you describe yourself? Don't take too long to figure out your current emotional state. The first answer that comes into your head is probably the right one for you.

3: Okay, that's your current happiness quotient.

4: After you are done with experiments #3 and #4 (a week) check out your, post experiment, happiness quotient. Are you a happier person than before? Yes? Good, you are on the right track. No? Figured out why? Skeptical? Be open and give yourself a chance. It will do you a lot of good.

Now let's get on to the next experiment.

Experiment 2: The "Before" and "After" Photos Test

If you are realized, the beauty of your Self will shine through. People will notice your changed appearance. You will be glowing from within. So why not take "before" and "after" photos to check this out. The differences you notice will motivate you to stay the course.

1: Pick an uncluttered spot for your photo shoot, either in front of a blank wall or a door.

2: Make sure that you are in an area that has light shining directly on you, and not coming from behind.

3: Take your "before" and "after" pictures at the same time of day.

4: Use the same camera. Different cameras will give varying results.

5: Before you start experiment #3, take two photos- your face and the entire you, from head to toes, close enough to see some details. Look straight ahead, and smile if you want.

6: Upload the photos to your computer and place them in a folder marked with the date. Name this folder- **BEFORE.**

7: After a week of self realization, take your "after" photos in the same way as you had done earlier.

8: Upload these photos to your computer and place them in a folder marked with the date. Name this folder- **AFTER.**

9: Check out these photos. Is there a difference in your appearance? Without telling your friends about your experiment, ask them to spot any differences in the "before" and "after" photos. Did they spot the difference?

Experiment 3: The Body of Light Exercise

It's time to get acquainted with the real you (Self). Let's start-

1: Stand in the middle of a slightly darkened room. You may try this exercise in a sitting or sleeping position, too. There's no problem with that.

2: Tense every muscle of your body, starting from your foot and ending with your face, for a few seconds and release the tension. Repeat this a few times until you feel sufficiently "loosened." You are relaxed now.

3: Close your eyes and direct your gaze to the spot between your eyebrows. Visualize a dot of sparkling, bright light there.

4: Now visualize this dot as slowly expanding into an egg shaped ball of light permeating our entire body.

5: Let this ovoid ball of light protrude in all directions from your body. Choose how large you want your BoL to be.

6: Think you are no longer a body made of flesh and bones. This luminous body is your true Self. You are powerful, immortal, unborn and supremely blissful. Experience this feeling.

7: Stay in this position for a while and enjoy the powerful sensation. Be happy you have recognized your true, powerful Self. I am willing to bet on this, you are going to feel a great change in you. The feeling's out of this world, seriously!

8: Initially, don't overdo it. After a few minutes, open your eyes.

9: So, this is the real you. How did you feel? Don't ponder over this. Carry on your regular activities as before.

10: Carry out this exercise for the next two days.

Experiment 4: Being your real self

Are you ready to move in this illusory world as the Self and not the physical body? Would you like to experience the sense of power and happiness when you do so? Yes? Go ahead!

1: Did you try out experiment#3 for three consecutive days? If yes, then you have now become acquainted with your real Self. If no, then do it before your proceed further.

2: It's time to move out in the illusory world as your true Self and not as a physical body with all its worries. Perform the **BoL exercise** and cocoon your physical body with the BoL.

3: You will be going out in the real world as your true Self. Imagine at all times that you are the BoL and not your physical body. Observe how people view you in your new Self.

4: I guarantee that people are definitely going to see you in a new light (pun intended). They're going to be amazed by your changed appearance. Their behavior's going to change.

5: Note down your observations at the end of the day. What are your observations?

6: Complete experiments #1 and #2 to test your progress.

Experiment 5: Silencing the mind

It's your mind which has created this illusory world. Instead of you (Self) controlling the mind, it's the other way around. You have been forced by the mind to take a part in this material world which has caused you much unhappiness. It's your turn now to silence the mind and try to control it. The following exercise will help you silence your mind a great deal, instantly. If you still hear some background noise, try to ignore it. It's your mind trying to break the silence. Perform this exercise whenever you need to stay calm and relaxed.

1: Sit in a comfortable position.

2: Keep your eyes closed.

3: Start by taking a long deep breath.

4: Exhale this breath after holding it for a few seconds. Do this a few times.

5: Let go of the surface tension in your body.

6: With your eyes closed, direct your gaze to a spot between your eyebrows.

7: Touch the tip of your tongue to the roof of your mouth.

8: Sit in this position for a while and feel the deep sense of calm engulfing you.

That's it! You have silenced the mind to a perceptible degree.

Open your eyes and figure out how you felt before / during and after you performed the above exercise. Do you feel a perceptible change?

Experiment 6: Mind feedback

You have learned how to silence your mind's continuous chatter. You will now train your mind to obey your commands and also learn how to receive feedback from your mind regarding the task assigned to it.

1: Sit in a comfortable position.

2: Close your eyes and breathe deeply for a few seconds.

3: Perform the **BoL exercise**. You are now the Self not the physical body.

4: Do the above **mind silencing exercise**. This should calm your mind.

5: Address the mind with the following words, "I am the Self and you are my mind. Henceforth, you will do my bidding. If I need anything in this material world, I will ask you to get it for me. You will obey me and carry out my commands. Does this make sense?"

6: You should hear a favorable reply from your inner voice. If you don't hear your inner voice, try again. After you receive the mind's assent, continue, "Mind, if and when I give you a specific task to perform, please tell me whether the task is doable or not."

Duh? What's this? There are occasions when the mind would not want to perform a certain task or it has some other plans. Or, due to previous conditioning, it might doubt it's abilities of creation. So, start with smaller tasks. As the mind becomes comfortable with its abilities, jump to bigger ones. Be gradual. Don't worry over the outcome! You will receive.

Experiment 7: Mind Control

It was the collective mind's idea to create these illusory universes and force you (Self) to play along. You have been totally subjugated. It's time you turned the tables on your mind.

1: Every morning after you wake up, sit on your bed with your eyes closed.

2: Breathe deeply and perform the **mind silencing exercise**.

3: Perform the **BoL exercise**. You are now the Self not the physical body.

4: Address the mind with the following words, "I am the Self and you are my mind. Henceforth, you will do my bidding. If I need anything in this material world, I will ask you to get it for me. You will obey me and carry out my commands. Does this make sense?"

5: You should hear a favorable reply from your inner voice. If you don't hear your inner voice, try again. After you receive the mind's assent, continue, "Mind, remember I am your master and you are my helper. Your duty is to obey me, serve me and make me happy."

6: It will take days before the mind finally realizes its place within you. After that, start expecting miracles. Whatever you wish, the mind will try to fulfill it for you!

TESTING THE POWERS OF THE SELF

If you have diligently performed the **BoL exercise** for a week, you are going to experience a great change within you. You will feel powerful and peaceful. You will feel secure because now nothing can hurt you and you are the most powerful being in the universe. You know that you can create, change or erase anything you want with your mind. You are able to remain detached from this illusory world because of this knowledge. You have now realized that this universe has been created by you. You are no longer a prisoner to the ups and downs of this illusory material world. You are unique. You will have total peace and happiness.

You are the Self. You are God. You are the creator.

Isn't this empowering?

Convinced?

No?

I am seriously going to be at odds with Ashtavakra here. He had no intention of using the awesome knowledge, given in the Ashtavakra Gita, to manifest anything in this world. However, most of us are not as enlightened as he was and probably will never be.

In order to validate his theories we need to conduct some tests involving the Self and mind in different situations. I understand that hankering after material possessions, love interests, sex and status should not be our only goal in this cosmic opera. Be detached. Be a spectator. Be happy that the real you (Self) is the creator of this illusory universe and you are really not in want of anything.

Huh? I have had enough. Now show me results……..

Okay! Let's check out the powers of your mind!

1: How to manifest physical objects

In this experiment, you are going to test your mind's awesome powers of manifestation. It's advisable that initially you should start small like small amounts of cash, appliances, mobile devices etc. As the mind becomes comfortable with its abilities, move onto larger objects like cars, houses, boats etc. Be gradual with your wish list.

I am sure you are going to be skeptical whether you will really receive what you have willed your mind to bring to reality. Remember, what I told you about you (Self) and your mind's powers. Believe.

1: Sit in a comfortable position.

2: Close your eyes and breathe deeply for a few seconds.

3: Perform the **BoL exercise**. You are now the Self not the physical body.

4: Do the **mind silencing exercise**. This should calm your mind.

5: Address the mind with the following words, "I am the Self and you are my mind. Henceforth, you will do my bidding. If I need anything in this material world, I will ask you to get it for me. You will obey me and carry out my commands. Does this make sense?"

6: You should hear a favorable reply from your inner voice. After you receive the mind's assent, continue, "Mind, I need you to manifest the following thing (be specific about what you want to the last details. You should be able to visualize clearly what you want.), please tell me whether this task is doable or not."

7: If your inner voice says "Yes" then tell your mind to go ahead. Don't force your mind by telling it that you want your desired object in a certain way and at a certain time.

8: If you feel that your mind is not comfortable with this particular task, inquire if there's an alternative object which it could manifest for you. Give your mind the freedom of choice.

9: That's it. Now chill. Don't ponder about the how's, why's and the when's. You will receive what you have asked as soon as your mind gets to it.

2: How to attract your soul mate

Let's be clear on this. Never use your powers to force a specific person to love you. It's volition of free will. Yes! It's quite possible to bring such a person in your life but the end result will not bring you happiness. That person was not in your script in the first place at all. Always focus on the qualities you want in your mate. So, don't be vague. Suppose you want a nerdy but highly sexed girlfriend who loves to travel, then, tell your mind about it.

After making this wish, don't hanker for instant results. When you start worrying about the outcome, all negative feelings begin to seep in. This blocks your mind's power to manifest. So, after you have asked your mind about your desire, just forget about it. Your mind has registered your desire and will work on it. Believe!

If you become impatient and begin to date someone else and this person begins to occupy your personal space, you are surely going to overlook the person you had wished for. You might not be able to recognize your soul mate, when that person appears before you, because you were so busy with your current date. The person of your dreams will walk away even before you know he / she was there. Be patient. Allow your mind to fulfill your wish.

Permit me to lecture a bit on my favorite subject- **detachment**. Have you ever noticed that when you think about a person for a nanosecond and forget about it, you are most likely to bump into that person in a short while? If, on the other hand, you keep thinking about a person deeply, you never get to see that person. In the first case you were detached while with the latter you were attached and obstructed the minds powers of creation. That's the power of detachment for you!

Shall we start?

1: Sit in a comfortable position.

2: Close your eyes and breathe deeply for a few seconds.

3: Perform the **BoL exercise**. You are now the Self not the physical body.

4: Do the **mind silencing exercise**. This should calm your mind.

5: Address the mind with the following words, "I am the Self and you are my mind. Henceforth, you will do my bidding. If I need anything in this material world, I will ask you to get it for me. You will obey me and carry out my commands. Does this make sense?"

6: You should hear a favorable reply from your inner voice. After you receive the mind's assent, continue, "Mind, I need you to manifest me my soul mate or companion (be specific about what you want to the last details. You should be able to visualize clearly what you want.), please tell me whether this task is doable or not."

7: If your inner voice says "Yes" then tell your mind to go ahead. Don't force your mind by telling it that you want your soul mate in a certain way and at a certain time.

8: If you feel that your mind is not comfortable with this particular task, inquire if it has someone else on its sights, which it could manifest for you. Give your mind the freedom of choice.

9: That's it. Now relax. Don't ponder about the how's, why's and the when's. You will receive what you have asked as soon as your mind gets to it.

3: How to heal yourself

When we talk about healing do we mean healing of the physical body or of the mind?

Is there a connection between the mind and sickness?

From ancient times to this century, it has been accepted that the mind can affect the course of sickness and it was believed that the mind needed to be treated simultaneously to accelerate the healing process.

I bet you must have heard of cases where the patients have cured themselves of cancer and other dreaded diseases overnight by changing their thinking process.

So what does this suggest?

Your mind is the creator of sickness and good health! It has the power to cure you of all your ailments!

As I have been saying, ad nauseam, the Self led by the mind have created this universe and have been playing various roles for millions of years. As time passed on, each mind began playing the game in its own unique way. This mental conditioning became the cause of disparities in the roles played by the minds and also having an effect on the physical body which it inhabited. Negative mindset resulted in sickly and loser roles while those physical bodies created by positive minds were always lucky and healthy. Even if they suffered adverse conditions or fell sick, their positive minds ensured their recovery. It's the state of the mind which determines your good health or illness.

If you are able to rid your mind of the accumulated "garbage", accumulated since the beginning of this cosmic opera, you can be free of problems and sickness permanently. You can achieve a state of permanent health and happiness.

In order to heal the mind and hence the body, you need to eliminate negative thoughts and replace them with positive thoughts. You need to impress upon the mind to set itself right and correct its perspectives in order to be happy and healthy.

If you are suffering from some illness or disease you should not discontinue medical treatment or surgical procedure prescribed, until your doctor says so. Carry out the following exercise in conjunction with your doctor's treatment to hasten recovery or to prevent a sickness reaching the stage where a surgical procedure becomes necessary. Your mind will help you and you will be free from your ailment very quickly.

Let's begin:

1: Sit in a comfortable position.

2: Close your eyes and breathe deeply for a few seconds.

3: Perform the **BoL exercise**. You are now the Self not the physical body. Imagine the BoL completely dissolving away all sickness and problems. Concentrate on the image of your body as completely healed and in the nature of light.

4: It's time to condition our mind. Perform the **mind silencing exercise**. This should calm your mind.

5: Address the mind with the following words, "I am the Self and you are my mind. Henceforth, you will do my bidding. If I need anything in this material world, I will ask you to get it for me. You will obey me and carry out my commands. Does this make sense?"

6: You should hear a favorable reply from your inner voice. After you receive the mind's assent, continue, "Mind, I need you to cure me of this ailment (be specific about your medical problem) please tell me whether this task is doable or not."

7: If your inner voice says "Yes" then tell your mind to go ahead. Don't force your mind by telling it to cure you by a certain time. It knows! Tell your mind to remove all thoughts of illness it has harbored over the ages and never let them return. This will ensure your mind having healthy thoughts and you not falling sick in the future.

8: It's also possible the mind will say, "No." It is perhaps signaling you to ask it another day. If it does, then continue with your medical treatment. When you instinctively feel that it's okay to go ahead then contact your mind and follow the above steps.

8: That's it. Don't ponder about the how's, why's and the when's. Your problems should disappear as soon as your mind gets to it.

4: How to change your present situation

Have you ever pondered over these questions?

Why is it that some people are very successful and others not?

Why are some people billionaires, while the majority live ordinary lives?

Why do some people live happy, healthy and contented lives?

I could go on and on……

You guessed right! It's our mind which is responsible for all this.

The mind has been responsible for creation of this illusory world and now become a prisoner of its own creation. Due to its attachment to the Game of Life (**http://ASIN.cc/1Q7_D9W**), you (Self) led by your mind have been playing different roles over millions of years. Somewhere, the plot got changed. Some minds developed a positive, successful attitude and their "physical" bodies became successful, lucky and rich. Other minds stumbled and thus the bodies created by them were not able to play successful roles. If you belong to the "not so successful" category, then it's time to change your role for the better. You are going to ensure that your mind changes its programming.

Stop playing loser roles. You don't deserve it. Be a winner. Let's change.

1: Sit in a comfortable position.

2: Close your eyes and breathe deeply for a few seconds. Start with the **mind silencing exercise**. This should calm your mind.

3: Perform the **BoL exercise**. You are now the Self not the physical body. Imagine the BoL completely dissolving away all the negativity and bad luck. Concentrate on the image of your body assuming a successful role in this soap opera.

4: It's time to condition our mind. Address the mind with the following words, "I am the Self and you are my mind. Henceforth, you will do my bidding. If I need anything in this material world, I will ask you to get it for me. You will obey me and carry out my commands. Does this make sense?"

5: You should hear a favorable reply from your inner voice. After you receive the mind's assent, continue, "Mind, I am tired of playing this loser's role (be specific about your present condition) and I need you to give me a complete, successful makeover. I want to be rich, good looking, successful (whatever you want to be. Be specific). I insist!

6: Don't force your mind by telling it to change you by a certain time. It knows! Tell your mind to remove all negative, loser thoughts it had burdened itself over the ages and never let them return.

7: That's it. Don't ponder about the how's, why's and the when's. You will be a changed person as soon as your mind gets to it.

5: How to handle problematic people at the office

Have you ever handled difficult, unpleasant and problematic people (your boss, your colleague, a client or anyone associated with your work / business) at your office or workplace? I am sure you have.

It's not directly possible to change the behavior and attitude of difficult people because we have no control over their behavior. However, we can use the power of our Self and the mind to bring about subtle positive changes at the office and workplace.

Here I go again. This universe and everything in it, including your dysfunctional office, has been created by our collective minds. It's your mind which has led you to play your current role in your office. Other minds, including those of the difficult, unpleasant and problematic people, are playing their individual roles. Everything's illusory. Don't join their group. Sit back as a spectator and watch. If you participate in their activities, then the dysfunctional behavior's just going to thrive. Be detached and functional.

Now let us use the power of our mind to bring about a positive transformation in the office.

1: Sit in a comfortable position.

2: Close your eyes and breathe deeply for a few seconds.

3: Perform the **BoL exercise**. You are now the Self not the physical body.

4: Perform the **mind silencing exercise**. This should calm your mind.

5: Address the mind with the following words, "I am the Self and you are my mind. Henceforth, you will do my bidding. If I need anything in this material world, I will ask you to get it for me. You will obey me and carry out my commands. Does this make sense?"

6: You should hear a favorable reply from your inner voice. After you receive the mind's assent, continue, "Mind, I need you to fill this office with feelings of calm, orderliness, good behavior and discipline. Talk to the other rowdy minds in this office and try to bring some sense in them."

7: Visualize your office or workplace filled with a bright light. Let this light engulf all the people in the room bringing about a positive transformation in them.

8: Be detached. Don't ponder about the how's, why's and the when's. You will soon notice positive changes at your office or workplace.

6: How to handle vicious people

Many a time, we are forced to deal with unpleasant, mean people in our illusory lives. They could be our relatives, associates or strangers. Don't we feel horrible when these people treat us unfairly, want to attack us or try various methods of disturbing our inner peace?

Remember these people are actually very insecure and secretly want to be loved and accepted. You are going to exclaim, "Are you kidding?" My reply is, "No." According to psychologists, these unpleasant individuals are actually crying for help and they are trying to make their feelings known by targeting you.

Fortunately, our new found knowledge will help us deal with this situation:

1: Don't panic: If you come face to face with such a person, don't panic. They will sense it and you will provide them the ammo to attack you. Take a few deep breaths and touch the tip of your tongue to the roof of your mouth. It will help calm you instantly. Don't try to fight back. It will only aggravate the situation. Try to be detached. Look detached. After all, this person is not real and cannot hurt you (Self).

2: Bubble of love and peace: After you have calmed yourself, try projecting a bubble, filled with love and peace, from your forehead and allow it to grow and completely engulf the unpleasant person standing in front of you. Believe it or not! In most cases it will have a positive effect on the targeted person.

3: Peace mantra: The ancient Indian texts have powerful prayers or mantras which a person can use for various purposes. There's this mantra "**OM SHANTI.**" The simple words of this mantra have awesome powers. If you are agitated, or facing a dangerous situation or person then try chanting this mantra. Believe the power of this mantra will help you tide over the problem facing you. It will!

7: How to deal with the fear of death

Are you afraid of dying? Don't be embarrassed to say "Yes." Seriously, the word "death" gives us goose-bumps. Even the gurus, who talk about the mysteries of life and death, secretly fear death.

Death is an eventuality in this game of life. What is born dies. It's impossible to escape the clutches of death.

What dies at death?

Is it your physical body or you (Self)? If you have read some of the pages of this book, you will have definitely figured out the answer. If you are still in the dark then allow me.

This universe and everything in it, including all the people, animals, plants and other living creatures, are just illusions which have been created by our minds. This material world is a gigantic soap opera where the mind has forced the Self to play different roles. Our physical bodies are nothing but characters in this cosmic show. The collective minds who devised this play must have thought that playing the same role in the same physical body for millions of years would be utterly boring and so they must have put a cap on the life spans of the physical bodies. Let's have fun in different bodies. Let each mind decide when and how to "kill" its role and enact a new role in a new body. So each physical body has its own life span set by the mind. After the stipulated time, it dies. The Self and the mind leave this "dead" body to be born again in a new body. This cycle of life and death has continued, for millions of years, on the various planets of this and other universes. The ancient Hindus called it **"reincarnation."**

If you or a person close to you is terminally ill or close to death please don't panic and think everything's over. You (Self) and your mind are immortal and never going to die. Think of death as a role change. You are discarding this worn-out body and donning a new one with its own set of experiences.

There's also an added bonus. The collective minds have also created illusions on the higher planes too. After death, you will experience the sensation of going through a tunnel and the presence of an incredibly bright being of light. This being showers profound love and compassion putting the "passed on" soul at ease. Others have experiences of meeting deities they worshipped while in their physical bodies, dead relatives or friends and beautiful surroundings. Those who have played highly negative roles experience horrific scenes after death. Barring a few stray horror cases, the transition period from the death of one physical body to occupying a new body is a pleasant experience.

So, why fear death?

If you have decided to participate in the illusory Game of Life and Death (**http://ASIN.cc/1Q7_D9W**) then try to get a successful new role. Tell your mind that since you (Self) and the mind are going to leave this body and take on a new body, you would want to play a successful, happy role. Be very specific about what you would need in your new role. Where would you like to be born? What would you like to born as? Have you any role models in mind? Figure out all possibilities. Take a paper and pencil and jot down what type of body you would like to have to the last detail. Visualize your new perfect body and surroundings. Please make this your dominant thought till you pass over. Your mind will take a role as suggested by you. **Say no to loser roles!**

If you heed Ashtavakra's words, you should not agree to play this game of life at all. Rein in your mind at the time of death and refuse to play a fresh game. **Merge with the infinite consciousness where you will be supremely blissful.**

There's one more thing I need to caution you strongly- Even if your life sucks, don't ever think of **suicide**. It's not the gateway to a new life. One of the rules of this life-death game is – No taking yours or others lives! Your next role will be even more terrible than this one.

So, live it out. This miserable life has given you an opportunity to be totally detached. Perform the **BoL exercise** daily. Think of yourself as the Self which is beyond this stupid mind game. The problems you are facing are your mind's problems and not yours. Ask your mind to solve this problem and create a better script for yourself.

You have a right to be happy. Ask for it.

Part II
ASHTAVAKRA GITA

ASHTAVAKRA AND KING JANAKA

King Janaka was the king of **Videha, India** and father of **Sita**, spouse of **Lord Rama** of the epic **Ramayana**.

According to legend, **Ashtavakra**, while an unborn child in the womb of his mother, became well versed in the **Vedas**. The Vedas, meaning knowledge in **Sanskrit**, are the oldest scriptures of Hinduism. They were supposed to have been revealed to mankind by **Lord Brahma**, the god of creation.

There are four categories of the Vedas:

The **Rigveda** contains hymns which are recited by the "presiding" priest;

The **Yajurveda** contains formulas which are recited by the "officiating" priest;

The **Samaveda** has formulas to be sung by "chanting" priests;

The **Atharvaveda** is a collection of hymns, spells, chants and incantations.

Ashtavakra would listen when his father, Kahoda, a renowned Vedic scholar, used to recite the Vedas loudly. Once day, the unborn child found some errors in the Vedic pronunciations of his father and he softly pointed out the errors to his father. Kahoda was an egotistic man. He was not delighted that an embryo was trying to be one up on him. His anger knew no bounds. He cursed his unborn son, "You think you are too smart, don't you? Be born with eight-fold deformities and let's see how you live with that." The curse took effect. Very soon, Ashtavakra was born with eight-fold deformities. Ashtavakra, in Sanskrit, means eight-fold, and thus he was christened with that name.

King Janaka was a scholarly person and he loved discussions about religion and spirituality. He used to arrange contests, with the scholars in his kingdom. The winner would be rewarded with immense wealth and the losers were thrown in a big well.

Twelve years passed and Ashtavakra grew up to be an enlightened soul. One day, his father, Kahoda, was invited to the court to participate in the contest. All the scholars were supposed to compete against, **Vandin**, the undisputed winner of many previous contests. Vandin was so well versed in religious and spiritual topics that he was able to easily defeat all the scholars in the kingdom, including Kahoda. As per the rules, the losers were thrown into the well. Actually, this well was a doorway to **Varuna**, the god of water and oceans' kingdom. The god wanted these defeated scholars to perform a sacrifice for him, which would take many, many years to complete. After completion, he was to set them free after rewarding them for their participation.

Since Kahoda did not return home, Ashtavakra went to the king's palace to inquire about his father's whereabouts. The king was busy discussing philosophy with the scholars. On seeing the deformed form of Ashtavakra, the entire assembly including the king burst out laughing. Ashtavakra also responded by guffawing loudly. There was complete silence. Everybody was perplexed. Instead of freaking out, this guy was laughing back at them.

King Janaka inquired, "Hey! Why are you laughing so loudly? What's the joke?"

Ashtavakra retorted, "O king, I thought I was amongst learned men but I find only court jesters here. What were you guys laughing at? My exterior deformed body or the immeasurably beautiful soul which lies within?"

The king and his group of scholars were tongue tied. This guy was talking sense. They had forgotten their true identity. They were attached to what they were seeing in the physical world, which was perishable, and not the indestructible world of the soul.

Ashtavakra continued, "O king, I have come to debate with your champion, Vandin, and if I win, please release my father."

King Janaka consoled Ashtavakra by assuring him that his father would return soon. If he was interested he could test his wits with Vandin. Ashtavakra readily agreed and the contest began. Vandin was duly defeated in the philosophical debate and thus he was thrown into the well. (If you are curious about the contest, check out my book "**Game of Illusions**" http://ASIN.cc/ytWryA)

His father, Kahoda, came out of the well with a bagful of riches and he was delighted to see his son had caused Vandin's defeat.

Kahoda returned home with his son. Very soon, they went to the river **Samanga**, where Kahoda asked his son to bathe in it. Ashtavakra emerged from the river with all his deformities gone. He was now a normal person. But he was stuck with the name, Ashtavakra. Ha!

Ashtavakra became a favorite of King Janaka and he would regularly visit the palace for discussions. These discussions are written in the form of dialogue, between the sage and the king. The result of these metaphysical discussions is the Ashtavakra Gita.

The original Ashtavakra Gita has 20 chapters. I have tried to be concise and so my version has only 11 chapters.

Read what Ashtavakra and the king has to say and ponder over their discussions. Perhaps, you, too, will have some new insights like I did!

1: Instant Liberation

King Janaka: O, wise one, how can an ordinary person attain wisdom? How does salvation come? How does he achieve renunciation?

Ashtavakra: Interesting question! If you want wisdom, salvation and renunciation, then you need to strictly avoid things which affect your senses. You must be forgiving, compassionate, honest, content and straightforward in your dealings.

If you stop identifying yourself with your body and know that you are actually pure consciousness, you will become truly happy, wise and serene. All these feelings- happiness, sorrow, love, sin etc., are attributes of your mind and not of your true Self. You are neither the doer, nor the enjoyer of these actions. Remember this and you will be free.

If you think this universe and everything within it is real, you become bonded to this idea and will never be free.

Keep affirming, "I am the non-dual pure consciousness." Abandon all sorrows associated with the material world and you will be blissful. Meditate on this aspect whenever possible.

Don't be bound by the fetters of your ego and I am again repeating this- You are an immortal, all pervasive, actionless, desireless, unattached soul who's an uninvolved witness to this illusory universe.

You are in reality pure consciousness. So, don't be a prey to your mind's desires. Remember everything in this universe, which has form (matter), is false. The formless (Self or soul) is changeless and immortal. If you know this truth, then you will be free from this cycle of births and deaths. You will attain salvation.

2: What's real?

King Janaka: You have told me something very profound. Previously, I would identify myself with this material world not knowing it was illusory. I was deluded! I realize now that this universe and everything in it is the creation of my mind. I understand that I am the Supreme Self (Soul).

Just as the waves and foam of the sea waves are not different from the sea water, the universe created out of the Self is not different from it.

Just as sugar pervades the entire fruit juice, I (Self) too, pervade the universe created in me, inside and outside.

An ignorant person thinks that this universe is real just as he would mistake a piece of rope, dangling from a tree, for a snake. With knowledge, the universe which has manifested from within me will disappear just like the wave into the water and the ornament into the gold.

I should be happy that I am actually beyond this universe. When it vanishes, I will be still there.

Everything in this world- the knower, the knowledge and the object of the knowledge has no existence. These have become manifest due to my ignorance.

There's neither bondage nor salvation for me. Everything's illusory. I am neither this body nor is it mine. I am the Self and I am forever free.

Ashtavakra: You nailed it, O, king. If you know the true nature of your Self then where's the necessity for earning fame and fortune in this world?

Due to our stupidity, don't we all run towards a glittering object thinking it to be gold or silver? Similarly, due to ignorance of the Self, aren't we attracted to all the illusory material objects thinking it to be real?

If you have figured out that the universe streams forth from your mind, like the waves of the sea, then why do you hanker after it?

If after knowing that you are pure consciousness then why do you crave sex and be part of all problems which accompany it?

If you are a part of this universal consciousness then why are you so miserable?

If you accept this world to be illusory then you will neither be happy nor distressed with the happenings of this world. You will not be frightened of death or calamities. You will become truly powerful.

3: The Power of True Knowledge

King Janaka: I was truly ignorant. This knowledge is awesome. Tell me more.

Ashtavakra: You are right, O, king! There's no comparison between an ignorant person who is burdened with worldly problems and the knower of the Self who plays his / her part in this life.

If you recognize your true Self then you are not burdened by worldly troubles. An enlightened person remains untouched by the duality of virtue and sin just as the smoke which rises up cannot touch the sky.

It's actually very difficult to figure out this knowledge but once this sinks in, the possessor of this knowledge becomes fearless. An awakened person realizes that this universe is nothing but the creation of the collective minds!

4: The Dissolution of Consciousness

King Janaka: What is "laya' or the dissolution of consciousness?

Ashtavakra: If you know your true Self, then what's there to renounce? If you have figured out that your body and this universe is illusory, then you can undertake the dissolution of consciousness.

Just as a wave becomes part of the ocean, try to rein in your mind along with your desires and make them a part of you (Self).

Just as the universe, though visible, is dissolved in your non-dual self and vanishes, try to dissolve your consciousness in the same way.

Never be affected by pleasure or pain, hope or disappointment, life or death.

King Janaka: It's not as easy as it seems.

Ashtavakra: There's no need to try what I have said. Even those seekers who are on the threshold of enlightenment fear the dissolution of individuality and body senses. Such an individual is afraid of losing the ego sense.

However, if you think you are the ocean and the universe its waves, then there's no need for renunciation or dissolution of the consciousness.

If you are able to figure out the difference between a glittering object (our universe) and gold or silver (Self) then with such understanding there's neither rejection nor acceptance of the dissolution of the consciousness.

If you realize that you are a part of the universal consciousness then with such understanding there's neither rejection nor acceptance of the dissolution of the consciousness.

With this knowledge, it's irrelevant whether you accept or reject the dissolution of the consciousness.

5: The Limitless Ocean of the Self

King Janaka: I've a few of my observations, too.

King Janaka: I have a few of my observations, too.

There are three types of deluded souls. I have figured out how they can attain enlightenment-

1: The first type believes in duality- the Self is different from the universe, both of which are real. These souls can remain established in the Self by thinking they are a vast ocean on which the ship of the universe moves along driven by the wind of the mind.

2: The second type believes in qualified non-dualism that though the Self and the universe are both real, the universe is a part of the Self. Such souls can achieve enlightenment by considering themselves as an infinite ocean on which the waves rise and disappear without causing any loss or gain to the ocean.

3: The third type believes that the Self is the only reality and this universe is but a false superimposition on the Self due to ignorance. In such cases, the soul should consider itself as a ripple-less ocean where the universe has been superimposed by imagination just like the magicians tricks. It's just an illusion.

O, Guru, I have said enough. Why are we so bonded to our creation even though it's illusory? Please enlighten me about it.

6: Bondage and Freedom

Ashtavakra: Bondage is a fascinating subject. It's the result of our mind attaching itself to the sense organs. Bondage takes place when the mind desires or grieves over something; feels happy or sad over a situation; accepts or rejects something.

It's the mind which has made the Self a prisoner and subject to all miseries including births and deaths. If the Self is able to shake off its attachment to the mind-body combination and remain a dispassionate witness to all the events within him and around him then it will regain its lost freedom.

Where there's no ego there's freedom; where there's ego there's bondage. Freeing oneself from the mental imaginations of happiness, sadness, ego, competitiveness, lust and other feelings without judging them as good or bad, right or wrong will unshackle you from your self-imposed prison.

That's it! In reality there's neither true bondage nor liberation. They're the delusions of the mind.

Remember your true identity (Self) and recognize the Self, residing in other entities, which have created this universe and all material objects with your collective minds.

This creation has hypnotized you to be its slave. Remove this delusion and you will be free.

O, learned guru! I've now understood what bondage means and what we need to do to be free. You've piqued my interest. Please continue.

King Janaka: Yes! I totally agree! There's no question of either bondage or liberation as these are mere delusions of the mind.

This universe is but a mental creation of the collective Selves and minds. This universe is a part of us and all miseries and sufferings are due to our sense of duality where we see the universe as not a part of us.

O, learned guru! I have now figured out what bondage means and what we need to do to be free. You have piqued my interest. Please continue.

7: Indifference

Ashtavakra: Thank you for your kind words. I am happy that I have been able to impart this spiritual knowledge to you. I will now be discussing indifference.

Is it surprising that there're a few souls in this world who have extinguished their passion for living / worldly pleasures after watching the miseries of mankind?

These individuals have realized the illusory qualities of our universe and become totally immune to the ups and downs of the world. Such persons do not indulge in lust or passion towards anybody.

The true knower knows that the Self is only real and part of the infinite consciousness. The rest including our universe and material objects are just illusory and products of our mind.

Such a person becomes peaceful and indifferent to the worldly activities.

He is truly the master of the universe!

King Janaka: Awesome! Please continue…..

8: Dispassion

Ashtavakra: O, king, learn to forego desire and stop striving for wealth and prosperity. Such tendencies have no limit and make our mind restless.

Look upon your spouse, children, houses, wealth, position and friends as a scene from a show or a dream which vanishes after you wake up.

Nothing's permanent in this world.

This universe is not real but a creation of your mind.

So, why go through all this pain to be one up over others.

Stop!

King Janaka: It's clear why people are so unhappy in this world. No one's truly satisfied. Even the richest people in the world! They still feel inadequate. There's no limit to one's ambitions! If everybody realizes the futility of their desires, then there would be happiness all around.

O learned one, you have taught us a simple solution to be happy but many won't buy it. We've been conditioned since our present and past births that this world is real and you need to succeed in it and take part in its various activities.

I, totally, believe what you have said so far. I am listening.....

9: Pure and Radiant Self

Ashtavakra: Your opinion makes total sense. It's very difficult to change our mindset which has been conditioned since many births.

I might sound repetitive but I must say this- Be desireless and unattached to everything around you. Happiness, sadness, births, deaths, luck and misfortune are all unreal. They're the products of our mind.

You are the creator of this universe. You can manifest or erase anything in this world. When you are aware of this reality, why should you be attached to your creation which is surreal?

There's no need to look out for gurus to teach you about reality.

The only teaching you will ever need is-You are the Self. You alone exist. The universe is unreal and is a creation of the universal consciousness. If you know this, you will be at peace with yourself.

10: Supreme Knowledge

King Janaka: You have taught us an easy way to be free from bondage and be truly happy. There's no need to perform yogic or other meditative exercises, recite prayers or mantras, listen to guru-talk to achieve bliss and serenity of the Self.

All you need to do is to withdraw your mind from the objects of the senses and remember that your true Self doesn't require these unreal objects of distraction and misery.

If you wish to be truly happy then you should strive to be desireless, unattached with worldly things and just contemplate upon your inner Self.

If you control the activities of the body, mind and speech you will start experiencing supreme bliss. You will not be bothered by what's happening around you. If you have understood the true illusory nature of this world, you will be nonplussed about what's happening around you.

I am now following these principles and I am living in true happiness all the while. I am not like the gurus who preach wondrous things, but they themselves are miserable due to their attachment to their body, actions and inactions. I have become a dispassionate spectator to this illusory world and truly blissful.

I have figured out that I am the supreme Self and the creator of this universe (along with other souls). I have full control over my desires and thoughts. I am truly happy and free.

My present blissful condition can only be understood by a person who has also realized his / her true Self.

11: Awakening!

Ashtavakra: Bravo, king! You sure are a fast learner. An open minded person can easily grab these new ideas whilst a skeptical person might take years before sense dawns upon him / her.

A person who wants to succeed in this illusory world is averse to the idea of detachment from sense objects, even though it might cause him / her grief, at some time or the other.

It's very difficult to comprehend that you are not the body, nor the body is you. You are not a participant of this world. You are a pure, intelligent, powerful being. You are a witness to the creation of your mind (our material universe). You are the Supreme Self. You are God. You are the creator.

Try to recognize that there's the Self in all living beings and their collective minds (infinite consciousness) have created this material world. Be free of ego / possessiveness and be happy. We're all equal!

Why do you wish to be the prisoner of your creation? Nothing's permanent in this creation. Look at the body. It is born, lives for a short while and then dies. The Self within the body never dies. It's the immortal witness to this game of life. When you have realized your true Self, then why do you lament?

This universe is not different from you. It has arisen out of your mind. Are the gold ornaments different from the gold used to create them?

Know your true Self. Why do you identify with this world by saying, "I am rich", "I am powerful" and such? Does this not cause uneasiness in you?

Remain unattached and you will be truly happy and free.

There are very few souls who do not hanker after the enjoyment of things they possess (created) or after things they have not yet possessed. They do not run to the forest, gurus or monasteries in search of the truth. Even though they eat, sleep and carry out various earthly activities, they remain detached and unmoved by the ups and downs of life. Such persons are truly blessed because they are contented with what they have. They are aware that these possessions are nothing but temporary creations of their mind and can change anytime as per their wishes. With this thought, an enlightened person becomes detached to all material possessions and remains free from any bondage.

King Janaka: O sage! Everything's clear now.

The only reality in this world is the Self which resides in all of us and is a part of the universal consciousness. The mind is the creator of this universe and the Self has become a prisoner of its own creation.

I have realized my true inner Self and so all doubts about existence and non-existence, unity and duality, reality and illusory etc., which are the products of the mind, have disappeared.

When the supreme truth is known to us, do we need to ponder over these questions?

- What is meditation, pleasure, prosperity or discrimination?
- What is Unity or duality?
- Where is time, past present or even future?
- Where is space, or even eternity?
- Who is God?
- Who am I (Self)?

- What is good, evil, happiness, sadness, fear, bravery, distraction or stillness?

- What is sleeping, dreaming, waking or procreating?

- What is life and death?

- What are the elements, the body, the organs and the mind?

- What is knowledge or ignorance?

- What is bondage or freedom from desire?

- What is "I", "this", "mine"?

- Where is the beginning or the end?

- Where is the origin or end of thought?

- What is creation and destruction?

- What are the ends and the means?

- What is activity or inactivity?

- What are the principles, universal laws and scriptures?

- Who is the disciple or teacher?

- What is the reason for life?

- What is existence or non-existence?

I don't think so. I think I have said enough!

Ashtavakra: (smiled) I agree!

THANK YOU!

Thanks for buying my book. Did you love it? If you enjoyed the book, please spread the word and leave a review on Amazon. Your opinion matters to me. Word-of-mouth publicity is crucial for any author to succeed. I would appreciate just a sentence or two.

Please leave your review here
http://www.amazon.com/dp/B00KXYSEO2

http://ASIN.cc/ychKfq

Thanks for any help you can provide to get the word out!

Please visit my Amazon Author Page

http://Author.to/MikeNach

MY BOOKS

If you liked this book, you will also love these books. Get them and be enlightened.

HOW TO BE THE MASTER OF THE UNIVERSE
http://ASIN.cc/ychKfq
 https://www.createspace.com /5034839

Game of Illusions
http://ASIN.cc/ytWryA
 https://www.createspace.com /5042255

Game of Life
http://ASIN.cc/1Q7_D9W
https://www.createspace.com/5344252

HOW TO GET ANYTHING YOU WANT? MAKE A MAGICK MIRROR!
http://ASIN.cc/RahVJf
https://www.createspace.com/5040665

How to Be Enriched in Every Way
http://ASIN.cc/12Jo4zL
 https://www.createspace.com /5065824

THE 40 PARABLES OF INVESTING
http://ASIN.cc/11ujpiL
 https://www.createspace.com /5029013

I CHING OF THE STOCK MARKET
http://ASIN.cc/bxxqcL
 https://www.createspace.com /5069717

WHY ME?
http://ASIN.cc/e5qS5f

THE HARE AND THE TORTOISE -BEAT THE BULLIES!
http://ASIN.cc/mocBz0

The Little Book That Beats the Bullies
http://ASIN.cc/12QD6kW
 https://www.createspace.com /5043967

DATING ADVICE: 30 Frequently Asked Questions
http://ASIN.cc/V_YBvf

Made in the USA
Lexington, KY
03 September 2015